D0128462

valentine treats

valentine treats

recipes and crafts for the whole family

by sara perry with kathlyn meskel

photographs by quentin bacon

CHRONICLE BOOKS

SAN FRANCISCO

Text copyright © 2001 by Sara Perry.
Photographs copyright © 2001 by Quentin Bacon.
Illustrations copyright © 2001 by Ellen Toomey.
All rights reserved. No part of this book may be reproduced
in any form without written permission from the publisher.

Sculpey III is a registered trademark of Polyform Products Company Inc. Hot Tamales is a registered trademark of Just Born Inc. Raisinets is a registered trademark of Nestle's USA Inc. Confections Division. Good & Plenty is a registered trademark of Hershey Foods Corporation. M&M's is a registered trademark of Mars Inc. Saran Wrap is a registered trademark of S.C. Johnson & Son, Inc. Oreo is a registered trademark of Nabisco, Inc.

Library of Congress Cataloging-in-Publication Data:

Perry, Sara.
    Valentine treats : recipes and crafts for the whole family / by author, Sara Perry.
    96 p.   22.2 x 20.4 cm.
    Includes index.
    ISBN 0-8118-2592-2 (pbk.)
    1. Valentine decorations.   2. Valentine's Day cookery.   I. Title.
TT900.V34 P47   2001
745.594'1—dc21   99-088462
                         CIP

Printed in Hong Kong.

Craft development by Kathlyn Meskel
Craft styling by Christina Wressel
Food styling by Darienne Sutton
Illustrations by Ellen Toomey
Photographer's assistant: Tina Rupp
Designed by Carrie Leeb and Laura Lovett
Composition by Suzanne Scott

Distributed in Canada by Raincoast Books
9050 Shaughnessy Street
Vancouver, British Columbia V6P 6E5

10 9 8 7 6 5 4 3 2 1

Chronicle Books LLC
85 Second Street
San Francisco, California 94105

www.chroniclebooks.com

Notice: This book is intended as an educational and informational guide. With any craft project, check product labels to make sure that the materials you use are safe and nontoxic. Nontoxic is a description given to any substance that does not give off dangerous fumes or contain harmful ingredients (such as chemicals or poisons) in amounts that could endanger a person's health.

Acknowledgments and Thanks

To my cherished friends at Chronicle Books, especially my editor Leslie Jonath, who suggested this book in the first place, and who encouraged me to cook and write about my favorite holiday. Thanks also to Mikyla Bruder for her valuable help and enthusiasm on every aspect of this book.

To Oregon-at-heart friends, Jane Zwinger, Catherine Glass, Larry Kirkland, craft goddess Debbie Lewis, Ken Hoyt, David Chen, Karen Brooks, Bette Sinclair, and Ben Merrill, who are always there to help with good ideas and great taste. And to Bruce Aidells, who taught me how to *really* cook meat with his book *The Complete Meat Cookbook.*

table of contents

happy valentines!

It's a magic moment when a valentine arrives, addressed to you. Personal, funny, thoughtful, sweet, evocative, hopeful, faithful, and passionate, love is there, just under the fold, ready to delight you with its message. To adore and be adored is one of life's deepest pleasures. Valentine's Day is a day for sweethearts, young and old, for love, and for friendship. It's a chance to surprise and delight someone special with just the right words, thoughts, and actions.

This heartfelt holiday began as an ancient Roman festival called the Feast of Lupercalia. The February night before the fun began, young women would write love notes, place them in an urn, and wait for a young man to select one. When he did, the two would become partners for ritual dances and, perhaps, something more. (The urn was chosen to hold these romantic messages since it was an early symbol of the human heart.)

In A.D. 496, Pope Gelasius named February 14 as Saint Valentine's Day and the Church gave the feast its liturgical blessing. Just which St. Valentine the Pope was honoring is still unclear. It seems there were two legendary Christian martyrs by that name who died on that day. The first was a third-century priest who defied Roman rule by performing marriage ceremonies for single soldiers. The second Valentine was a physician beheaded for his Christian faith. In his prison cell, he wrote notes that he signed "From your Valentine." One reached a little blind girl whose sight was miraculously restored when she opened his card.

Valentine's Day flourished in the Middle Ages when valentine verses and greetings became popular as ballads. Handmade paper valentines began to appear in the 1400s, and lovers found all kinds of ways to get their messages across. Verses in which the first letters of the lines spelled out a lover's name were popular, as well as those in which a tiny picture would take the place of a word (an "eye" for an "I"). Folded puzzles were also the rage. In the nineteenth century, prim and proper Victorians found Valentine's Day the perfect excuse to allow uninhibited love to blossom, through lavish cards made with lace and ribbons.

Valentine's Day remains one of our favorite single holidays. More cards are sent, more chocolate hearts are consumed, and more fragrant bouquets are enjoyed (and dinner-for-two reservations made) than on any other day of the year. When I met and fell in love with my husband, Pete, it seemed like Valentine's Day lasted for months. I treasured every ticket stub, every envelope covered with doodles, and every wish-you-were-here postcard with Bob Dylan's lyrics and Pete Perry's poems. As our family grew, so did the traditions around this happy day. Handmade cards. Favorite music. A backyard bouquet in the mailbox. Special meals based on our favorite recipes. And, best of all, a surprise Valentine's Day any month of the year.

The Valentine's Day crafts and recipes in *Valentine Treats* are ones my family knows and loves, and I know you will love them too. The instructions are written in recipe form, and are designed to delight both children and adults. The introductions offer many suggestions for working together and having fun. Valentine's Day is about being with those you love, in person and in spirit. *Valentine Treats* makes that easy.

tips for cooking with kids

art box basics

- ♥ construction paper, assorted colors
- ♥ craft glue and white glue
- ♥ crayons and colored pencils
- ♥ decorative scissors, or pinking shears
- ♥ felt-tipped pens and markers, assorted colors
- ♥ glue sticks
- ♥ paintbrushes
- ♥ paints (acrylic, tempera, or watercolor)
- ♥ paper punch
- ♥ pencils
- ♥ resealable bags of beads, stamps, and trinkets
- ♥ ruler
- ♥ scissors, round-nosed for safety
- ♥ stickers, assorted

♥ Go over the whole recipe before you begin. (You can ask an older child to read it out loud.) Check to make sure you have all the ingredients and utensils you'll need.

♥ Select a clear kitchen counter, one with enough space to spread out everything you'll need, and be sure to clean the counter before and after you cook.

♥ Make sure everyone washes his or her hands with soap and water. (Did you know that doctors and nurses scrub their hands for a full 15 seconds to make sure they're clean?) A sneeze? A cough? Cooking dinner and handling raw meat or poultry? It's time to wash those hands.

♥ Tie long hair back so it won't cloud vision or fall into the food.

♥ Store sharp knives and cooking tools in a safe place until they are needed. Wash knives, graters, and peelers separately. If they are all together in soapy water, someone might reach in and get cut.

♥ Have oven mitts handy to remove a hot dish from the oven or the microwave.

♥ Don't set pots on the stove top with the handles sticking out. Kids—and adults—can easily bump into them.

♥ Be sure children are careful around hot stoves or grills and that they know what to do if there is a fire. If grease catches on fire, smother it with a lid or baking soda. Never use water. Always have a fire extinguisher in working order in the kitchen and make sure older children know how to use it. Double check that every child knows how and when to dial 911.

tips for crafting with kids

♥ Read through the Art Box Basics and Around-the-House Supplies, and stock up on the basics in advance. Keeping supplies in a plastic storage container or shoe box will help make getting started easy.

♥ Select a work space. Craft projects can be messy, so choose a spot that's easy to clean up, well lit, and well ventilated. Make sure there is a solid, flat surface on which to work that's big enough to accommodate the project you've selected.

♥ Use waxed paper or a disposable dropcloth to cover the work surface. Have paper towels and a damp sponge on hand for quick cleanups.

♥ Read through the project instructions before getting started. Your kids can help collect the needed materials and arrange them on the worktable, ready to use.

♥ Lay a few simple ground rules. Everyone will have a good time if he or she knows what is expected. Encourage the creative juice to flow, but divide responsibilities and cleanup fairly.

♥ Review safety precautions. Go over how craft supplies and tools are handled. Explain why some tools, such as knives and scissors, should be used only by an adult.

♥ Protect clothes with smocks, oversized T-shirts, or aprons. Better yet, turn an old set of play clothes into craft clothes.

♥ Let Cupid's helpers work at their own pace and skill level. The most precious creations are often a bit crooked or colored a little outside the lines. Remember that the magic and fun is in the doing.

around-the-house supplies

♥ adhesive tapes, including invisible and masking

♥ aluminum foil

♥ clear plastic storage bags and twist ties

♥ garden clippers

♥ manila file folders

♥ paper towels

♥ paring knife

♥ saucers and small bowls

♥ scratch paper

♥ sponges

♥ waxed paper

Cupid, draw back your bow, and let your arrow go . . . straight to the heart with these Valentine's Day hearts and cards. Be right on target when your Heart-to-Heart Paper Garland magically appears in just the right spot, or a Say-It-with-Hearts Valentine delivers its message.

valentine hearts and cards

In this chapter, you'll discover crafts simple enough for your cherubs to express their sweet intentions with lots of sticker and stamp fun, and handfuls of home-made hearts just right for friends and family. You'll also find plenty of ways to enchant your sweetheart with secret (and not-so-secret) Lost and Found Hearts. And everyone will get the point across with an elegant Pushpin Valentine.

Whether you and the kids turn the dining room into a Hearts-in-the-Making assembly line or you make a secret-admirer valentine behind closed doors, take aim, have fun, and let the hearts fall where they may.

heart-to-heart paper garland and greeting card

Paper garlands always add a festive touch wherever they appear, and they also make the most romantic greeting cards. You can write, print, or stamp your feelings, one at a time, across each garland heart. Then fold the hearts together, accordion-style, and tuck them into an envelope. When you mail your hearts, be sure to add "please hand cancel" to the envelope (so they aren't crushed) and enough extra postage.

8½-by-11-inch sheet card stock, handmade paper, or construction paper

3-inch heart cookie cutter or free-form heart (facing page)

pencil

scissors

ruler

paper punch

6 lengths complementary sheer ½-inch ribbon, raffia, or string, each 12 inches long

6 lengths complementary sheer ½-inch ribbon, raffia, or string, each 24 inches long

Makes one 24-inch (⅔-yard) garland

Lay the paper flat on a clutter-free work surface. Position the template close to the paper's edge, and using the pencil, lightly trace it. Repeat to create seven hearts. Use the scissors to carefully cut out each heart.

Using the ruler and paper punch, mark and punch two holes, one on each side of the heart, approximately 1 inch from the top and ¼ inch from the side. (With a template heart you can measure and punch the first heart, and use it as a pattern.) Repeat with each heart.

To connect the hearts, thread a 12-inch ribbon length through the right-hand hole of one heart, then back through the left-hand hole of another. Pull the ribbon until both threaded hearts meet at the ribbon's center, and tie in a bow. Repeat, until all the hearts are connected.

To add ribbon lengths for hanging, thread one 24-inch ribbon through each outer heart's outside hole. Adjust each ribbon to its center point, tying in a bow. Use the remaining ribbon for hanging.

the perfect heart

Whether it's drawn or traced, cut or copied, or found in the guise of a leaf or pebble, the perfect heart is always in the eye of the beholder. There are many ways to make a heart to share. Whatever way you choose, however your favorite boys and girls end up making their valentines, here are some handy tools and techniques to help you.

cookie cutters: Heart-shaped cutters are inexpensive and come in a variety of sizes, making them perfect patterns. Trace the outside edge lightly in pencil and the heart will be ready to outline with colorful marking pens, or cut out with scissors.

patterns and stencils: Make your own patterns and stencils by simply folding a piece of paper in half and lightly tracing half a heart shape along the fold. Cut along the outline, and you are ready to unfold the heart. The cutout heart becomes the pattern; the remaining paper becomes the stencil. Inexpensive precut plastic patterns and stencils are available where craft and scrapbook supplies are sold.

stamps: Heart-shaped stamps are available in a wide variety of styles and designs at art supply, craft, stationery, and discount stores. You also can make your own heart-shaped stamps. Use scissors to cut kitchen sponges, and you'll create soft lines and impressionistic hearts. Use a craft knife to score a heart shape into an art gum eraser or potato half. Carefully cut around the design about 1 inch deep until the surrounding eraser/potato falls away. Use acrylic paint, 2 tablespoons at a time, poured into a saucer for stamping.

old valentines: Last year's valentines make great heart-shaped patterns for decorating this year's cards. Use the whole design, or snip out favorite heart bits to cut and paste a heartfelt collage.

hearts in the making

It's a toss-up which is more fun, making Valentine's Day hearts or receiving them. For cherubs of all ages who want to play Cupid, here are some ways to make hearts turn and love blossom.

conversation hearts

Using brightly colored card stock, cut out a handful of hearts. With medium felt-tipped pens in complementary colors, add cheery chat and loving labels to each heart, such as You're Cute, Love You, Big Hug, Best Pal, E-Mail Me, and Be My Icon.

special delivery

Cut out fifteen 1-inch hearts, using one color card stock. (I like deep red or bronze.) Write a Valentine's Day message on a 2-by-3-inch note card, then tuck both the hearts and the card into a 4-by-6-inch envelope, ready to deliver. To let your love show, instead of using a standard envelope, try one in vellum and write the address with a permanent felt-tipped marking pen.

antique valentines

Thanks to color photocopying, you can turn a single antique Valentine's Day card into a mailbox full of love notes. Use a glue stick to lightly tack three or four antique cards to an 8½-by-11-inch card stock sheet, and photocopy. Carefully cut out the copied designs, then add them to hearts, cards, or packages. Note: Due to copyright laws, many photocopy stores restrict copying newer Valentine's Day cards.

say-it-with-hearts valentine card

Three rows of three hearts, nine ways to say "I love you." It's that simple.
(Though it sometimes seems so complex.) On a creamy background,
cutout hearts in decorative paper utter love silently. Two tiny red hearts,
placed side by side, also speak for young followers of Valentine cutting
out hearts for the first time.

Makes 1 card

Position the card stock lengthwise on a clutter-free surface, and set the
envelope aside. To mark the card's outside edge, using the ruler and
pencil, measure and lightly draw a line 1½ inches from the paper's top
edge. Lightly draw another line 1 inch from the paper's right-hand edge.
Use the scissors to carefully cut along the marked guidelines. Fold the
card in half widthwise, creasing it along the folded edge.

Make the decorative heart template by first drawing a 1½-by-1-inch
heart on the cardboard. Cut out the template, making sure the edges
are smooth. Trace the heart pattern three times onto each sheet of
decorative paper, then carefully cut out all nine hearts.

Arrange the hearts on the greeting card's front panel, in three rows,
each with three hearts. Leave a ½- to ¾-inch border around the card's
outside edge, as well as a ½- to ¾-inch space between each individual
heart and each row of hearts. Use the glue stick to attach each heart.
Allow the glue to dry completely, about 1 hour. Add a Valentine's Day
message, and send with love.

8½-by-11-inch sheet white
or cream card stock, and
matching 5¼-by-7¼-inch
envelope (or purchased plain
note card with envelope)

ruler

pencil

scissors

3-by-3-inch piece light
cardboard

3 sheets assorted decorative
paper, each 4 by 6 inches

glue stick

valentine tags

Reminiscent of classic shipping tags, these heart-shaped message-makers are a unique way to say, "I'm sending my heart to you." You and your children can trace and cut out the hearts with ease. Punching the holes and applying the self-sticking hole reinforcements is the most fun for the elementary school crowd.

Pssst: *Want a sure-fire way to keep the after-school TV off? Along with the supplies to make the tags, include stickers, stamps, bits of lace, and simple charms. These tags look great decked, trimmed, and embellished by budding artists. Kali, my middle-school neighbor, came up with another idea. She cut out a 6-inch heart, punched holes all around its perimeter, and made a lace-up toy for my three-year-old grandson, Dylan.*

Lay the file folder open on a flat surface. Using the pencil and scissors, lightly trace or draw twelve 2- or 3-inch hearts on the open folder, and cut them out. Use the paper punch to make a hole at the top, about 1/2 inch in from each heart's indentation. Encircle the hole with two hole reinforcements, one on each side of the heart. Fold a 14- to 16-inch length of string in half, and thread it through each hole without pulling it all the way through. Bring the string's two open ends through its folded loop, pulling them until the loop tightens. After writing a sweet greeting or a To/From message, attach the strings of your heart to the package.

You will need:

plain manila file folder

pencil

scissors

paper punch

self-sticking hole reinforcements

white cotton string

pushpin valentines

pencil

4⅛-inch-by-5-inch sheet
   tracing paper

8 blank white or cream note
   cards, each 4⅛ by 5 inches,
   with matching envelopes
   (often available in boxed sets)

3 paper clips

old magazine

T-pin

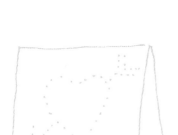

Use this simple piercing technique on plain note cards to create simple and elegant valentines you can send to your friends. Or, turn it into a family project where everyone makes one or more cards, and be sure to include the artist's initials on the back, where the logo would go. To complete the gift, tie the stack with a ribbon for someone's special "pin pal." Older children can do this craft on their own, even down to selecting other simple shapes to duplicate. Younger children will need help positioning the design and using the T-pin.

Makes 8 note cards

To make the pattern, use the pencil to sketch or trace a simple 3-inch design, such as a flower, rocket ship, or heart and arrow, onto the tracing paper. Open a note card and position the tracing paper, right side down, on the card's inside flap, so the top edge meets the card's center fold. Make sure the design is positioned as it should appear on the card. Use the paper clips to fasten the card and tracing paper together.

Place the opened card onto the magazine, pattern-side-up. Following the pattern, use the T-pin to evenly pierce holes, spaced ⅛ inch apart, through both the tracing paper and card. When the entire design has been pierced, carefully remove the tracing paper and clips. Using the same tracing paper, repeat with each remaining note card.

personal best

Use the pushpin technique to add a name or initials to note cards, or to the top of plain stationery. Remember to turn the traced letters so that they appear backwards through the tracing paper.

lost and found hearts

Like love, hearts can be lost and found in the most unexpected places. A cluttered drawer conceals a stack of old love letters; a garden path reveals a heart-shaped stone; a weekend flea market offers heart lockets, charms, and buttons. Wherever you or your kids look, you're sure to find hearts.

There are lots of ways to show off your discoveries: Let your kids glue, staple, or sew them with a simple stitch to a note card. Place the found treasures on a tray to make a centerpiece. And don't forget those secret love objects, known only to the eyes of beholders: a cafe receipt; an envelope with doodles; his fountain pen; her key-ring charm. You'll invent others . . .

- ♥ heart-shaped stones

- ♥ a rose petal, indented in the center

- ♥ a lipstick kiss on anything

- ♥ a heart-shaped locket, charm, or button

- ♥ 2 or 3 seashells, placed "just so"

- ♥ a stack of love letters tied with a ribbon

- ♥ a heart-shaped mosaic of tiny dried rosebuds

- ♥ an aspen, birch, or lilac leaf, turned upside down

- ♥ last night's ticket stub

- ♥ tonight's reservation

- ♥ heart-shaped cookie cutters, molds, or baking tins

- ♥ suit of heart playing cards, laid open

Love's labors will not be lost when you create these valentine decorations and gifts. A special heart will beat faster when a Message in a Bottle delivers its secrets, and then skip a beat when a Sweetheart Candy Box reveals its treasure.

valentine decorations and gifts

Bubble up a storm with your favorite boys and girls when you make Burst-a-Bubble Painted Paper into stationery, postcards, and bookmarks for every heart on their list. Use the language of flowers to say "I love you" to your mom or best friend with a Simply Elegant Bouquet of fresh-cut flowers, wrapped, with a Victorian touch. Create a candlelight dinner for the love of your life with the jewel-like brilliance of Valentine Votives. The instructions you need for these and other gifts are all here in this chapter.

the glittering art of beaded wire

36 inches (1 yard) 26-gauge
   gold beading wire

8 to 12 transparent red
   heart-shaped beads, 10 mm

8 to 12 clear starflake beads,
   10 mm

8 to 12 red faceted beads,
   4 mm

With nothing more than simple wire and dime-store beads, you and your cherubs can dress up your home in valentine jewelry using a simple technique of threading the beads and tying the wires into sparkling garlands. Use them one at a time or twist them end to end. They'll keep their shape whichever way you form them. The more, the merrier.

Encircle simple votive candleholders or candlesticks for a festive family dinner; loop napkins with rings of sparkling beads; and toast those special memories with fanciful champagne flutes. Here are the instructions on how to make your glittering garlands.

Makes one 24-inch (²⁄₃ yard) garland

Lay the wire on a flat, clean surface. Thread a heart-shaped bead onto the wire, positioning it in the middle. Secure the bead by tying it in place with a half-knot. Add a starflake bead to the wire, tying it 1½ inches from the heart. String a faceted bead next, tying it 1½ inches from the clear one. Continue to add beads in this order, leaving 1 to 1½ inches between each bead and 2 inches of open wire at each end.

For longer garlands, connect two or more finished garland lengths by threading the wire tip from one finished garland through the end bead of another completed strand, using the end wire from each. Tie these wires with a secure half-knot, snipping any excess wire. Repeat the process as many times as necessary to create the desired garland length.

valentine votives and cupid's candlesticks

Imagine a festive family dinner glittering with romance and enchantment. Candlelight and beaded garlands are all the magic you'll need. You'll want to experiment with the number of garlands to use to create the look you want.

Begin by wrapping the garland's end wire in a loop around the votive holder or candlestick, near its base. Secure the garland in place by twisting the wire's tip around the garland at the point where they meet. Loosely wrap the garland three or more times around the votive holder (five or more times around the candlestick) to just below its top edge. Follow the same method to hook the remaining wire tip. Adjust the loops for a finished look.

For each votive, you will need:

1 or more beaded garlands

2-inch glass votive holder

For each candlestick, you will need:

1 beaded garland (facing page)

7-inch tapered candlestick

loops of love napkin rings

These sparkling, simple-to-make napkin rings add just the right detail to a Valentine's Day table setting. For a special touch, slip a printed quote on top of the napkin, and wrap the wire around it too.

In one hand, gather the napkin as if to insert it into a napkin ring. With the other hand, place the end of the garland in the middle of the gathered napkin, adding a quote if desired. Wrap the garland loosely around the napkin four or five times. To finish the ring, twist the wire ends around the garland, where they meet.

For each ring, you will need:

a clean napkin

1 beaded garland (facing page)

a printed quote (optional)

beaded champagne flutes for two

For each flute, you will need:

1 beaded garland (page 26)
a stemmed champagne flute

Start off the evening with pizzazz: toast your love, your kids, or the evening yet to come, with these fanciful flutes. They also make sensational containers for a shrimp cocktail or a decadent dessert.

Wrap the garland's end wire in a loop around the flute's stem where it meets the base. Secure the garland by twisting the wire's tip around the garland at the point where they meet. Loosely wrap the garland around the stem five or six times. Follow the same method to hook the remaining wire tip where the flute's stem and bowl meet. Adjust the loops evenly around the stem. After the flute has been used, remove the garland, and wash as usual.

it's a wrap

For each finished gift,
you will need:

a wrapped present
1 or more beaded garlands
    (page 26)
your choice of 2-inch-wide
    ribbons (optional)

To make any gift you wrap look "hooshed"—my friend Ken Hoyt's name for all things elegantly wrapped—add the unusual touch of a beaded wire garland. By itself, the look is elegant; in tandem with ribbons, it looks exquisite.

To wrap only with the beaded garland, encircle the wrapped gift with garland lengths just as you would with a ribbon. Tie a knot to secure the wire, then bend the remaining lengths into the shape of a simple bow, securing the wire loops at the knot. If you're using ribbon, wrap the gift with the ribbon first and make a lavish bow. Finish by loosely weaving the garland in and out of the bow.

burst-a-bubble painted paper

Your preschool cupids will have as much fun blowing the bubbles as you will making the printed paper. This is a great family project. After mastering one color, everyone will want to try creating marbled magic by repeating with a second color. (See Marvelous Marbled Magic, page 30.)

Makes twelve 6-by-9-inch printed pages

Cover a clutter-free work area with two long sheets of waxed paper, overlapping them by 2 inches. (For quick cleanups, make sure paper towels and a moist sponge are within easy reach.) Place the pie plate on the protected surface. With a slotted spoon, combine the bubble liquid and paint, stirring until well blended. (The solution will be about $1/4$ inch deep.)

Place the drinking straw in the bubble mixture. Have your little helper gently blow through the straw until bubbles cover the liquid's surface. To create smaller bubbles with a tighter pattern, use the straw to stir the liquid.

Holding a piece of the watercolor paper by the edges, carefully lay it flat on the bubbled surface so that some of the bubbles break. Do not let go of the paper or let it touch the liquid. Lift the paper straight up, away from the solution. Set the paper, paint-side-up, to one side. Blow fresh bubbles, and use the same technique to print the paper a second time. Repeat four to seven times, until the paper is completely marbled with the bubble design. Use the same technique to print the remaining paper.

Lay the finished paper face up on a flat surface to dry. Drying time will range from 2 to 4 hours, depending on the saturation and thickness of the paper. If a lighter paper is used, the edges may curl. To flatten, place the dry sheets under a large book or stack of magazines.

continued

waxed paper

pie plate

slotted spoon

1 bottle (4 ounces) bubble liquid (see note)

2 tablespoons red tempera paint

drinking straw

6 sheets watercolor paper, each 9 by 12 inches, cut in half widthwise

Note: You can make your own bubble liquid by adding 1 tablespoon clear dishwashing detergent to 1 cup water. After the project is complete, the remaining bubble paint can be poured into a container and stored for up to 1 month.

marvelous marbled magic

For a sophisticated look, much like that of faux-marbled papers found in specialty shops, double the amount of bubble liquid, dividing it between two pie plates. Add 2 tablespoons umber craft paint to one dish and 2 tablespoons metallic gold craft paint to the other. Proceed as directed, covering each sheet with umber bubbles. Repeat with a light coating of bubbles made from the gold solution. (Since watercolor paper absorbs quickly, you don't have to wait for one color to dry before applying another.)

everything-in-one notes

For 6 notes, you will need:

6 sheets bubble-art painted paper (page 29)

6 self-adhesive stickers or seals

This is another perfect grown-up present that your children can create with minor supervision from you. They'll love blowing the bubbles and choosing just the right envelope stickers.

Turn bubble paper into a cheery note card that combines the stationery and envelope in one neatly folded piece. Use the plain side for the message and the gaily printed side for its pretty envelope. Seal with a kiss, and a sticker of your choice.

pixie postcards

After you cut the paper into postcards, let your young artists decorate the cards with stickers and stamps to give as school valentines, or wrap a bunch to give a favorite teacher, a relative, or a friend.

Use the ruler and pencil to measure and lightly mark the papers, each into two 4-by-6-inch cards. Use the scissors to carefully cut out the postcards along the marked lines. Decorate the bubble-art side with stickers or stamps. Use the felt-tipped pen and ruler to divide each post-card into message and address sections. Don't forget to make a "place stamp here" square.

For 6 postcards, you will need:

ruler

pencil

3 sheets bubble-art painted paper (page 29)

plain-edged or decorative-edged scissors

stickers or stamps

fine felt-tipped pen

bookmark the spot

He can mark a favorite passage; she can take up where she left off; and you can make their reading time begin with a smile when they catch a glimpse of their valentine bookmark.

Use the ruler and pencil to measure and lightly mark the bubble paper into three 2-by-9-inch strips. Use the scissors to cut the strips along the marked lines. Use the felt-tipped markers to add a name and valentine message to the back of each bookmark. For a charming finish, use a hole punch to make a hole at one end and add a loop of ribbon, decorated with a tied-on charm or bead if desired.

For 3 bookmarks, you will need:

ruler

pencil

1 sheet bubble-art painted paper (page 29)

plain-edged or decorative-edged scissors

felt-tipped markers

hole punch

ribbon

charms or beads (optional)

sweetheart candy box

waxed paper

1 empty heart-shaped cardboard
  candy box, 4 by 4 inches
  (make sure it is not the
  plastic kind)

glue stick

2 red heart-shaped doilies,
  each 4 inches wide

18 inches (¹⁄₃ yard) red or white
  wired ribbon, ¹⁄₂ inch wide

scissors

valentine cutout or decorative
  keepsake, 2¹⁄₂ by 2¹⁄₂ inches,
  optional

1 red or white construction
  paper or cardstock heart,
  3 by 3¹⁄₄ inches

Every February, variety stores and supermarkets stock their shelves with small, inexpensive heart-shaped candy boxes. You and your little helper can transform these candy-filled Valentine's Day classics into a magical memento holder or cookie container faster than Cupid can flutter his wings. (Be sure to enjoy the enclosed candy first.) You can use the liner paper as a heart template.

If you're looking for valentine cutouts to decorate your box, don't forget vintage valentines, magazine clippings, scrapbook cutouts, stickers, or color-copied photos of your favorite times and places.

Makes 1 box

Cover a clutter-free surface with two long sheets of waxed paper, over-lapping them by 2 inches. Place both candy box halves, open sides down, on the work area. Use the glue stick to lightly cover the lid. Carefully place one doily onto the glued surface, adjusting it so that the lid is covered and the edges are evenly matched. Repeat with the bottom half, using the second doily.

To decorate the lid, tie the ribbon into a bow, and apply glue to the bow's underside at the knot. Attach it at the lid's center point, just where the heart indents. Use scissors to evenly trim the ribbon ends. To add a cutout, use the glue stick to lightly outline its underside. Arrange the cutout on the box, pressing it gently into place. Let dry completely, 20 to 30 minutes.

To complete the box with a message label, center the paper heart on the inside of the bottom half, and glue it in place. (You can also use the same technique, and a slightly smaller heart, to add a surprise message on the inside lid.)

a simply elegant bouquet

The ancient Romans, the Druids, Shakespeare, and the Victorians all knew the power of the petal, and gave meanings to their favorite flowers. In the eighteenth and nineteenth centuries, tiny nosegays known as tussie-mussies were made up of flowers and herbs picked and arranged according to their definitions. Prim and proper Victorians found this a delightful way to send romantic messages, which flower dictionaries made easy to decipher. Whether you choose flowers for their beauty or the secrets they reveal, here are some ways to speak their language.

pure wrapture

For 1 bouquet, you will need:

flowers

natural twine or raffia

ruler

scissors

white butcher's paper

scotch tape

self-adhesive decorative sticker
  or seal

36 inches (1 yard) double-edge
  satin or grosgrain ribbon,
  $\frac{1}{4}$ inch wide

4-by-6-inch sheet note paper

Give a bouquet of flower-stand roses or market-fresh flowers a stunning presentation when you crease and fold crisp white butcher's paper with an envelope-style flap to protect the blossoms.

Select and arrange your flowers, setting one stem aside. Holding the flowers gently in place, wrap and tie the stems with a strand of the twine or raffia. Next, measure and cut a sheet of the butcher's paper into a square that is twice the length of the bouquet. Lay the paper on a flat surface so the square is oriented as a diamond. Position the bouquet in the center, with the paper's corner points to each side.

Fold the lower point up over the flower stems, creasing the paper in a straight edge 1 inch from the stems. Bring the left-hand point over the flowers, creasing the paper 2 to 3 inches from the bouquet. Repeat the fold with the right-hand point, including any overlapping paper from the other side. Secure with scotch tape. Carefully fold the open point,

continued

36

envelope-style, over the bouquet, making sure not to damage the blossoms. Secure the flap in place with the sticker or seal.

Lay the wrapped bouquet on a flat surface, positioning the single flower stem on top of the wrapping lengthwise. Secure with the ribbon, wrapping it around the packaged flowers at the midpoint. Tie tightly in a knot to create a waistband. Write a flowers-for-you message on the note paper. Roll the note into a small, tight tube and secure it to the package with the ribbon at the knotted point.

tussie-mussies

For 1 bouquet, you will need:

2 round white paper doilies, each 6 inches in diameter

scissors

flowers, including 1 rose, 6 inches in length

greens such as herb sprigs, artemisia, or santolina, 6 inches in length

1/4-inch-wide self-adhesive floral tape

36 inches (1 yard) satin or grosgrain ribbon, 1/4 inch wide

In the eighteenth century, these petite bouquets were carried for health reasons because it was believed that their perfume kept the air pure. Customs changed, and in the nineteenth century, fragrant tussie-mussies held romantic meaning. Today, this old-fashioned custom is an enchanting way to express your feelings to someone special.

To create a base for the bouquet, fold one doily in half, then in quarters. Continue folding this way to create a fluted effect. With the scissors, cut a hole in the doily's center. Repeat with the second doily.

Arrange your flowers and greens, placing the rose in the center. Holding the bouquet in place, slip the stems through the first doily. Trim the stems 1 to 2 inches at the bottom to create a point. At the base of the first doily, wrap and stretch the floral tape around the stems from top to bottom and secure. Slip the taped stems through the center of the second doily. To keep the doilies in place, wrap the ribbon twice around the stems at the doilies' base and tie into a bow.

the language of flowers

Create your own eloquent note with a single flower, or compose an evocative, witty, and very personal message by combining several kinds of flowers to make a brilliant bouquet or a secretive tussie-mussie. Here is a dictionary to guide you:

Chrysanthemum (red) "I love"

Clover "Think of me"

Daffodil respect

Daisy innocence

Fern sincerity

Forget-me-not true love

Hibiscus delicate beauty, grace

Iris passion

Ivy twines fidelity, marriage

Jonquil "Please return my affection"

Lavender devotion

Lilac (purple) "I'm falling in love with you"

Mint virtue, warm feelings

Pansy "I'm thinking of you"

Parsley merriment, festivity

Peppermint warmth of feeling

Rose love and all of its meanings (see below)

red rose "I love you," respect, courage

red rosebud purity, loveliness

bouquet of red and white roses unity, harmony

bouquet of red and yellow roses happy feelings, joy

yellow rose "Try to care"

coral or orange rose desire

pale colored roses friendship, comradeship

a single rose "I love you"

two roses joined to form a single stem "Will you marry me?"

blooming rose above two buds secrecy

Rosemary remembrance

Scented geranium happiness

Stock lasting beauty

Thyme daring, courage

Violet faithfulness

Zinnia "Thinking of you in your absence"

tips for love among the roses

Whether it's a single bud or a lavish bouquet of long-stemmed beauties, roses have always been the most popular flowers to give on Valentine's Day. As you can see in The Language of Flowers (page 39), a rose's color, shape, and combination with other roses can reveal much about love's passion and enthusiasm. Here are some tips for savoring roses' fragrance and making that message last:

♥ To condition your flowers for a long life, cut the stems at a 45-degree angle while holding them under water. Remove any leaves from the stems that will be submerged.

♥ Fill a vase two-thirds full with clean fresh water, adding flower food according to package directions, or use one crushed uncoated aspirin with 1 tablespoon granulated sugar per quart of water.

♥ For a full-blown rose bouquet, you can encourage your rosebuds to bloom by placing them 12 to 15 inches from a 100-watt bulb overnight. (The warmth and light helps them open.)

♥ When a cut rose starts to droop, keep it upright for an extra day or two by inserting a round-cut toothpick through the bloom's center down into the stem, snipping off any toothpick that shows.

♥ Dry your rose bouquet so you can savor the blooms for months to come. Enjoy the rosebuds. When they begin to open, take the flowers out of the water, remove most of the leaves, and cut the stems to about 10 inches. Bunch six to eight stems together and secure the ends with a rubber band. Hang by the rubber band upside down in a dark, dry, draft-free place like a closet or pantry. Allow three to six days to dry completely.

heart stoppers

One of today's great craft inventions has got to be heat-set clay. It's soft, pliable, and just plain fun, and it bakes to a bright, smooth finish. My five-year-old friend Jack Meskel thinks it's great to "moosh, and mash, and make dinosaurs," but that's for another day. Here, bright red clay (you could choose another color) is molded into hearts, then glued to a plain cork to create a fanciful stopper.

Makes 2 bottle stoppers

Divide the clay in half and roll each half into a ball. Set aside one ball. Starting at the first ball's center, work downward, molding the clay into a rounded point. Create the heart's top by making a slight indentation in the middle of the ball's rounded top. Mold and shape each side of the indentation to form the heart's upper half. Turn the clay often to keep all sides balanced and to prevent the heart from becoming flat on any one side. Repeat to make a second heart with the remaining clay.

Press the top of one cork into the side of one heart at the point they will connect, making an indentation in the clay about ¼ inch deep. Remove the cork, setting it aside. Place the heart on a foil-lined baking sheet. Repeat with the remaining cork and heart. Bake and cool the hearts according to package directions.

Cover a clutter-free surface with two strips of waxed paper, overlapping them by 2 inches. Cover the first cork's top end evenly with the cement, fitting it into the heart's matching indentation. Repeat with the remaining cork and heart. Set the finished stoppers aside to dry completely according to label instructions, generally 24 hours. Fill each bottle with your favorite elixir (bath oil, salad dressing, etc.), insert the heart stoppers, and your love potion is ready to give.

1 package (2 ounces) Red Hot Red Sculpey III Clay (or any thermo-set resin clay)

2 clean, empty clear glass bottles with clean fitted corks (such as vinegar or wine splits)

aluminum foil

1 baking sheet

waxed paper

1 tube (2 ounces) clear household cement

message in a bottle

Float this message out to sea, or give it as a gift to the one you love. Predict his future; write her a promise; or propose something even better.

There will be no question who your valentine is when you top the bottle with a bright red Heart Stopper (page 41). You also might think about decorating the outside of the bottle with hand-painted stencils, using acrylic paint. Or, let your cherubs loose with heart-shaped stickers.

Write your note on the paper. Wrap the paper tightly around the middle of the spoon handle, holding it in place with one hand. With the craft wire in your free hand, wrap the wire around both the note and the handle, working from one end of the note to the other. Leave ½ inch of the wire straight and unwrapped.

Making sure the paper stays inside the wire, carefully pull both the paper and wire off the spoon handle. Push the straight wire end into the bottom center of the heart stopper cork. Insert the corked message into its bottle.

You will need:

5-by-7-inch sheet of paper

wooden spoon with handle

18-inch length of 20-gauge craft wire

heart stopper cork and bottle (page 41)

"it's a frame-up" memory tray

A ticket stub, an invitation, the scrap of paper on which you first wrote his phone number. . . they all come together to make a gift that will take the two of you straight down memory lane. Here's a memorable tray for carrying treats when you're celebrating a special friendship, the magic of early romance, or your five-year-old's birthday.

Makes 1 tray

Remove the glass, paper, and cardboard backing from the frame. Place the cardboard backing on a clean, clutter-free surface, setting the other pieces aside. To create the tray's mat (the area surrounding the memorabilia), position the decorative paper on the cardboard backing so that all edges match. Using the glue stick, cover the paper's underside with an even coat, and press gently to seal to the cardboard backing.

To add a background for the memorabilia, place the decorative mat on the work area either horizontally or vertically, depending on which is to be the top of the tray. Center the plain background paper on the mat, gluing it in place. Using fingertips, smooth out any wrinkles, working from the center outward to the edges.

Arrange the memorabilia on the background. If the framed memorabilia is to be used only as a tray, it can be arranged in all directions; if it will be hung or displayed upright, it is a good idea to arrange the pieces in one direction, suitable for hanging. When all the pieces are arranged, use the craft glue to secure each piece in place. Let dry overnight, then reassemble the frame. Write a "framed with love" note on the back.

Note: Select a frame with wood that is 2 to 3 inches wide and has attractive lines and detailing. Remember, it is important that the frame can lie flat, since it will be used as a tray.

- 11-by-14-inch decorative wooden or gilt frame, without mat (see note)
- 11-by-14-inch sheet decorative fine-quality paper or hand-made paper
- glue stick
- 9-by-12-inch sheet complementary plain paper, heavy stock
- photographs, clippings, and mementos
- 1 bottle (2 ounces) craft glue, with applicator tip

two-for-the-show:
a night at the movies

6 cups popped (unbuttered) popcorn

1 theater-style popcorn bucket (see note)

1 cup candy conversation hearts

2 or 3 small boxes favorite movie-munching candy (such as licorice ropes, Hot Tamales, Good & Plenty, M&M's, or Raisinets)

movie passes, rented video (see note), and/or special certificates

24-by-24-inch sheet clear wrapping film

36 inches (1 yard) red satin or grosgrain ribbon, 1 inch wide

valentine tag (page 21)

Whether you rent the first movie you ever saw together or create the perfect date with movie passes and a certificate to your favorite bistro, here's a terrific way to set the stage and get the show on the road. Your kids will also think it's a super gift from a very cool parent, especially when the certificate spells "fast food."

Serves 2 nicely

Pour the popcorn into the bucket. Add the conversation hearts, and toss into the popcorn. Arrange the boxes of candy and the movie passes, video, or any certificates in the popcorn. Lay the wrapping film on a flat surface, setting the bucket in the middle. Gather up the four corners. Hold them in one hand, centered over the bucket. With the other hand, use the ribbon to tie the gathered film together just above the bucket's contents. Finish with a bow and tag.

Note: Theater-style, ready-to-pop popcorn buckets can be purchased at most video stores. If unavailable, use a white paper gift bag decorated with red stripes, scout flea markets and thrift stores for old film tins, or immortalize a plain cardboard box with a collage of movie advertisements, reviews, and promotions.

lavender bath salts

With only two ingredients, your bathing beauties can stir together this fragrant gift of soothing lavender bath salts. That's all you'll need for a long, luxurious, close-the-door, unplug-the-phone bath. Except maybe a child-free house, even for an hour.

To give as a gift, package the finished salts in a pint glass canning jar, a white paper Chinese-style take-out food container, or a clear cellophane gift bag. Add a handmade label and greeting, and finish with dried lavender sprigs tied with a raffia bow.

Spread 2 cups Epsom salts evenly in a the glass baking dish. Sprinkle the salts with 30 to 35 drops of the lavender oil, using your fingertips to blend them together. Remix the salts as they begin to dry and form a light crust, 10 to 15 minutes. Repeat this process three or four more times until the salts have dried completely and a crust no longer forms, about 1 hour.

You will need:

Epsom salts
9-by-13-inch glass baking dish
essential lavender oil

Love is a many-splendored thing, and so are the delightful sweets and treats you'll find within this chapter. There are Valentine Sugar Cookies, Razzle-Dazzle Hearts, and Chocolate Almond Sugar Hearts in all shapes and sizes. There are easy-to-make sweets like Secret Chocolate Cookie Truffles and Sparkling Fortune Cookies that

valentine sweets and treats

your kids can create at the kitchen table, and heart-shaped, savory pies, delectable at cocktail parties and a real treat for children anytime. You'll also find love potions to bring out the best in all of us. There's even a dog-gone great treat for your best friend—the one who gives you undivided attention, even when you're too busy to do more than pat his head.

The gifts you and your children make from the kitchen say "I love you" in the most thoughtful way and bring out the true meaning of Valentine's Day.

valentine sugar cookies

1½ cups all-purpose flour

¾ teaspoon baking soda

¼ teaspoon salt

½ cup (1 stick) butter, at room temperature

½ cup superfine sugar, plus more for sprinkling (or granulated sugar processed for 10 seconds in the food processor)

1 large egg, lightly beaten

1½ teaspoons vanilla extract

3 drops red food coloring

In my house, it's not a holiday without sugar cookie cutouts, and our Valentine's Day sugar cookies are some of best. I think it's because they're so cute and so easy to make. During the first week of February, whoever is home gets to help me cut out the various-sized heart shapes from the pink and white dough. Then we begin mixing and matching the sizes and colors to make lots of different patterns and designs. For an afternoon kitchen project, you'll want to make the dough ahead of time, so it will be chilled enough for you and your little sweethearts to roll out.

Makes about 2½ dozen cookies

In a bowl, whisk together the flour, baking soda, and salt.

In another bowl, use an electric mixer set on medium speed to beat together the butter and ½ cup sugar until light and creamy, about 5 minutes. Beat in the egg and vanilla, and continue to mix for 2 minutes.

On low speed, gradually add the flour mixture to the butter mixture until just combined. With lightly floured hands, gather the sticky dough into a ball. Divide the ball in half. Return one half to the bowl, add the food coloring, and mix until blended. With floured hands, form each half into a ball. Divide each ball in half, and flatten each half into a disk. Wrap each disk in plastic wrap. Refrigerate until firm, at least 2 hours or preferably overnight.

Preheat an oven to 375°F. Set aside the 2½-inch and 1- or 1½-inch heart-shaped cookie cutters, and two ungreased or parchment-lined baking sheets.

Remove one of the plain dough disks from the refrigerator. On a lightly floured board, on a pastry cloth, or between two sheets of heavy-duty plastic wrap, roll out the dough ¼ inch thick. (If it is too hard, let it rest for 5 to 10 minutes.) Use the 2½-inch cookie cutter to cut the dough into hearts. Use a spatula to place the dough on a baking sheet, leaving ½ inch between the hearts. Repeat rolling and cutting with one of the pink dough disks.

To create contrasting colors and patterns on each cookie, use the 1- or 1½-inch cutter to cut and lift out a smaller heart inside, or to the outside edge of, the larger heart. (The small heart will lift up with the cutter.) Pop out the dough with your fingertip, and replace it with a heart of the contrasting color. (Dough scraps can be combined by color and rerolled once, or both colors can be combined once to make marbleized hearts.) Sprinkle with sugar.

For soft cookies, bake until set but still pale, about 8 minutes. For crisper cookies, bake until pale golden, 10 to 12 minutes. Transfer to a wire rack to cool completely. Repeat rolling, cutting, and baking with the remaining chilled dough.

Variation: For flavored hearts, substitute 1 teaspoon of the vanilla extract with wintergreen, lemon, or almond extract. Continue as directed. For spicy hearts, add ½ teaspoon cinnamon, nutmeg, ginger, or Chinese five-spice to the other dry ingredients, and continue as directed.

tips for rolled cookies:

♥ Using superfine sugar creates a lighter, flakier cookie.

♥ Forming dough into disks instead of balls before chilling guarantees easier rolling.

♥ Rolling chilled dough between two sheets of lightly floured heavy-duty plastic wrap is an easy way for beginners to get good results (I use Saran Wrap). By lifting the bottom sheet, the cut shape will often pop right out, ready to transfer to the baking sheet.

razzle-dazzle hearts

Makes about 2½ dozen cookies

Razzle-dazzle your various valentines with these glittering red, sugar-crusted cookies. It's simple enough to do. Follow the Valentine Sugar Cookies recipe (page 52). Before baking, let your pixie Picassos use a clean watercolor brush to paint the large or small hearts with an egg-white wash (one egg white lightly beaten with 2 teaspoons water). Using clean fingertips or a shaker, carefully cover the wet, painted areas with red colored sugar. Continue as directed.

chocolate almond sugar hearts

Forget the chocolate bonbons. Instead, bake a batch of these buttery-rich chocolate shortbread cookies and stack them in a Sweetheart Candy Box (page 34) that you've made yourself. (You can use the box liner or a 2½-inch cookie cutter as the cookie template.)

Makes about 2½ dozen cookies

Follow the Valentine Sugar Cookies recipe (page 52). After creaming the butter and sugar, add 2 ounces melted and cooled unsweetened chocolate, and substitute 1 teaspoon of the vanilla extract with 1 teaspoon almond extract. Omit the red food coloring and continue as directed, using only the 2½-inch cookie cutter. Sprinkle with plain or cinnamon sugar (½ teaspoon cinnamon mixed with ¼ cup superfine sugar).

cinnamon candy sugar hearts

The only thing kids enjoy more than helping you make these candy-filled cookies is eating them. When the red cinnamon candy is crushed and baked, it melts, giving the cookies a "stained glass window" that's as yummy to eat as it is fun to peek through.

Makes about 2½ dozen cookies

Follow the Valentine Sugar Cookies recipe (page 52), setting aside two foil-lined baking sheets. Use a 2½-inch heart-shaped cookie cutter to cut the dough, and transfer the hearts to a baking sheet. Use a 1½-inch heart-shaped cookie cutter to cut and remove the center dough from each large heart. (This dough can be gathered and rerolled once.) Carefully place a rounded ½ teaspoon of crushed hard cinnamon candy in the center of each cookie. Bake until the candies melt and the edges of the cookies start to brown, 8 to 10 minutes. Cool slightly before removing from foil, or slip the foil off the cookie sheet onto a counter and let the cookies cool completely.

sparkling fortune cookies

I predict rave reviews when you serve these adorable fortune cookies, all dolled up for Valentine's Day with squiggles and patterns of sparkling colored sugar. I foresee kids having a blast painting and decorating the store-bought cookies, and breaking a few on purpose. ("What's your fortune say?") I also know that the cookies would make a great present for a friend, gift-wrapped in a clear cellophane bag with a few loose fortunes of your own.

Makes about 1 dozen cookies

In a small saucepan, combine the sugar and water. Bring to a boil, stirring until the sugar dissolves. Remove from heat, stir in the food coloring, and let cool. (By coloring the sugar syrup you'll be able to see where you've painted the designs.)

Pour 2 or 3 tablespoons of the colored sugar water into a small bowl or cup. Working with one fortune cookie at a time, dip the paintbrush into the syrup and paint patterns on the cookie's surface in sections. (Make sure to apply a medium coat.) After applying the syrup, hold the cookie over the tub and sprinkle the wet area with sugar. Lightly tap off any excess before moving to another section. To create a half sugar/half plain cookie, paint half and dip it into the tub.

After completing each cookie, place it on a wire rack to dry completely, up to 2 hours for patterned cookies, 4 to 5 hours for a solid coating. Store in an airtight container.

½ cup granulated sugar

¼ cup water

2 to 3 drops red food coloring

1 box (3½ ounces) purchased fortune cookies

Small paintbrush

1 tub (4 ounces) red sugar sprinkles, or your favorite color

secret chocolate cookie truffles

You will need:

semisweet chocolate chips

round chocolate sandwich-style cookies, such as Oreo cookies

mini heart icing decorations

colored sprinkles

I spotted these divine chocolate treats in an uptown candy shop along Chicago's Miracle Mile. They looked like huge truffles, each wrapped in cellophane with a tiny pink bow. Imagine my surprise when I took my first bite. These rich chocolates were entirely made out of two chocolate sandwich cookies stacked on top of each other and coated with semi-sweet chocolate. So simple, so good, and so easy to make. Your kids will have a great time creating these treats with your guidance, and surprising their friends with the secret insides.

In the top of a double boiler, over simmering water, melt the chocolate chips. Divide an equal number of cookies into two piles. Arrange one pile on a parchment-lined or waxed paper–lined baking sheet. Spread 1 teaspoon of the melted chocolate on top of each cookie. Stack a second cookie, from the other pile, on top. To set, place the baking sheet and cookies in the refrigerator for 15 minutes.

To coat each cookie truffle, remove the cookies from the baking sheet and place wire racks on the sheet. With clean fingers, dip and turn each cookie truffle into the melted chocolate. Allow the excess chocolate to drip back into the pan. Set the truffles on the wire rack to dry. To garnish, let the chocolate harden slightly, and top with a heart and sprinkles. Repeat with the remaining cookies.

These cookie truffles are best eaten within five days. With longer storage, the chocolate coating will begin to turn cloudy.

so-what-if-he-forgot
chocolate chip cookies

It's happened to all of us. No Valentine's Day card. No box of candy. Not even a phone call. That's the time to sink your teeth, and your feelings, into a big, delicious cookie, and here's the one that will fill almost every unrequited craving.

Makes about 4 dozen cookies

Preheat an oven to 350°F. Set aside two ungreased or parchment-lined baking sheets.

In a bowl, whisk together the flour, baking soda, and salt.

In another bowl, use an electric mixer on medium speed to beat the butter and sugars until light and fluffy, about 5 minutes. Beat in the vanilla. Add the eggs and beat until blended, about 1 minute. Add the flour mixture, 1/2 cup at a time, until blended and no flour shows. Add the coconut, pecans, chocolate chips, and toffee chips or raisins, if desired. Beat on low speed until blended. Add the oats, and continue to beat until blended.

Drop by rounded tablespoonfuls onto a baking sheet, leaving at least 1 inch between each mound of dough. For chewy cookies, bake until light golden, about 12 minutes. For crisp cookies, bake until golden brown all over, about 14 minutes. Cool slightly on the baking sheet before transferring to a wire rack, or carefully pull the parchment paper from the pan and place it, along with the cookies, on the wire rack. Repeat with the remaining dough. Store in an airtight container.

1 1/2 cups all-purpose flour

1 teaspoon baking soda

1 teaspoon salt

1 cup unsalted butter

1 cup granulated sugar

1 cup light or dark brown sugar, firmly packed

1 1/2 teaspoons vanilla extract

2 large eggs, lightly beaten

3/4 cup shredded coconut, firmly packed

1/2 cup toasted pecan bits

1 cup semisweet chocolate chips

3/4 cup white chocolate chips

1/2 cup toffee chips or raisins (optional)

2 1/2 cups old-fashioned rolled oats

heart and flower snacks and garnishes

An easy way to make healthy snacks fun to eat is to cut raw vegetables into bite-size treats, using heart- and flower-shaped garnish cutters. This method worked for my mom, and it has worked for me. Garnish cutters are a great addition to your kitchen props, and you'll find all kinds of uses for them. They're readily available in specialty cooking stores such as Williams-Sonoma, and often come in tins containing up to 12 different shapes.

On February 14, toss a handful of carrot hearts and jicama daisies into a sandwich sack for a lunch-box snack, or use them as salad garnishes or surprise additions to a chicken pot pie. For the next teddy-bear picnic, add a little color with toothpick spears of vegetable hearts. Make them all the same size using all the same vegetables, or switch them around for a crunchy rainbow treat.

Peel the carrots, cucumbers, and jicama, if desired. Slice each into rounds approximately 1/4 inch thick. To prepare the bell peppers, core and seed. Cut into quarters, and flatten gently with your palm. (When purchasing bell peppers, look for ones with flatter sides.)

Arrange the slices on a cutting board. Use heart- or flower-shaped cookie or garnish cutters that are slightly smaller in diameter than the vegetable slices. With the jicama and red pepper, you'll be able to cut more than one heart.

If they are not to be used immediately, place the hearts and flowers on a moist cloth or paper towel, cover with plastic wrap, and refrigerate for up to 3 hours.

You will need:

carrots

seedless cucumbers

jicama

red, yellow, or orange bell peppers

3/4-inch or garnish-size heart- or flower-shaped cutters

peanut butter with love sandwiches

2 slices sandwich bread

peanut butter

peanut butter partners such as fruit jams or jellies, fresh sliced bananas, honey, sliced gherkin or dill pickle, marshmallow cream, dried raisins or other dried fruits, granola, crisp bacon and cheese, chutney, lettuce (on all of the above!)

Surprise your lunch-box cherubs, or let them make their own favorite peanut butter sandwiches using large cookie cutters to cut sliced breads into fun shapes like hearts, teddy bears, or even dinosaurs. Have different types of sandwich breads available so that each sandwich slice can be a different color.

Makes 1 sandwich

Use a 5-inch heart-shaped cookie cutter to cut the bread slices in the desired shape. Spread one side of one slice with peanut butter. Choose your favorite peanut butter partner to cover the second slice. Press the fillings together, and you're ready to eat. If not, place the sandwich in a sandwich bag, or cover with waxed paper or plastic wrap until ready to serve.

heartland chicken pot pies

Pies are always a treat, and these are no exception. To celebrate Valentine's Day, the flaky pies are shaped into hearts you hold in your hands and pop into your mouth. The tender chicken filling goes together in a flash. This is comfort food at its best.

Makes 6 pies

To make the filling, in a bowl, combine the potatoes, chicken, carrot, peas, and cheese. Sprinkle the beau monde, garlic powder, salt, and pepper over the mixture and toss. Set aside. (Makes 1¾ cups.)

Preheat an oven to 375°F. Set aside a 5-inch heart cookie cutter or muffin cutter and two greased or parchment-lined baking sheets.

To make the pastry, in a bowl, whisk together the flour and salt. Add the shortening and use a pastry blender, two knives, or your fingertips to combine the mixture until it resembles coarse crumbs. Slowly add the ice water, stirring until the dough holds together. Do not overmix.

With lightly floured hands, gather the dough into a ball. Divide in half and flatten each half into a disk. Leave one disk out and refrigerate the other, wrapped with waxed paper or plastic wrap.

On a lightly floured surface, use a floured rolling pin to roll out the dough ⅛ inch thick. Use a cookie cutter to cut out hearts, collecting the trimmings to roll again. Use a spatula to transfer the hearts to the baking sheet, leaving ½ inch between them. Repeat with the remaining dough until you have twelve heart cutouts. Spoon about 3 tablespoons filling on top of six of the hearts. Place the remaining hearts over the filling. Use a fork to crimp the edges and poke a set of holes on top. Brush the tops with the melted butter.

continued

For the filling:

½ cup frozen shredded hash brown potatoes

½ cup (about ¼ pound) finely chopped uncooked boneless, skinless chicken breast

¼ cup grated carrot

¼ cup frozen petite green peas

¼ cup shredded Cheddar cheese

½ teaspoon beau monde seasoning

¼ teaspoon garlic powder

¼ teaspoon salt

¼ teaspoon ground black pepper

For the pastry:

2 cups all-purpose flour

1½ teaspoons salt

½ cup (1 cube) vegetable shortening, cut into pieces

½ cup ice water

½ cup melted butter for brushing

Bake until golden, 35 to 40 minutes. Transfer to a wire rack and cool until the crust is just warm to the touch. Otherwise, the filling can be too hot for children. Store in an airtight container in the refrigerator for up to 2 days. To reheat, preheat an oven to 350°F and bake uncovered until heated through, about 12 minutes.

mamasita's chicken filling

In a bowl, combine ½ cup frozen shredded hash brown potatoes, ½ cup finely chopped uncooked chicken (about ½ whole chicken breast), 1 can (4 oz) California green chiles, seeded and chopped, ½ cup shredded sharp Cheddar cheese, ½ teaspoon garlic salt, ½ teaspoon ground cumin, and ½ teaspoon chile powder, and continue as directed. Makes 1½ cups.

spicy beef and raisin filling

In a skillet, sauté ½ pound lean ground beef and ¼ cup minced onions in a frying pan over medium heat until the onion is limp and the meat browned. Discard the fat. Stir in 3 tablespoons raisins, 3 tablespoons chopped ripe black olives, ¼ cup tomato-based purchased or homemade chile sauce, 1 teaspoon chile powder, ½ teaspoon ground cumin, ½ teaspoon garlic salt, and ½ teaspoon ground coriander. Salt and pepper to taste, and continue as directed. Makes 1½ cups.

angel meringue cake

Growing up, my favorite holiday dessert was mom's Angel Lemon Pie. Her melt-in-your-mouth crust was actually a deep-dish meringue, and the filling was lemon curd folded into whipped cream.

I love the grand look of a tall cake, so I adapted her recipe to create a two-layer meringue confection. For Valentine's Day, we like to splurge and garnish the top with fresh raspberries imported from some sunny climate and tiny edible pansy blossoms. (When Matthew and Julie are helping me, we usually put on candy conversation hearts instead.)

If you've ever had trouble making a meringue, try this recipe. It's fool-proof. You'll be so pleased with the results, you'll be sending Valentine's Day wishes my way.

Makes one 8-inch cake; serves 6 to 8

Preheat an oven to 350°F. Set aside a parchment-lined baking sheet. Draw two 8-inch circles on the parchment, leaving at least 1 inch between them. (You may need to use two baking sheets.)

To make the meringues, in the clean bowl of a standing mixer fitted with a whisk, on medium-low speed, beat the egg whites until frothy, about 1½ minutes. Increase the speed to medium-high, add the salt and the vinegar, and slowly add the sugar, whisking until thick, about 2½ minutes. Increase the speed to high and whisk until stiff and glossy, about 4 minutes. Sprinkle the cornstarch over the whites during the last minute of beating. Divide the meringue between the parchment circles and gently spread out evenly within each circle.

continued

For the meringues:

6 egg whites, at room temperature

large pinch of salt

1½ teaspoons white vinegar

1½ cups superfine sugar

1 tablespoon cornstarch

For the mousse:

6 egg yolks

½ cup granulated sugar

juice and minced or grated zest of 2 lemons

½ cup unsalted butter

1 cup heavy (whipping) cream

fresh raspberries and edible blossoms such as pansies or small candy hearts for garnishing

Reduce heat to 300°F. Bake in the middle of the oven for 1 hour. Turn off the oven and leave the meringues inside, with the door shut, until completely cool, about 4 hours. The meringue will be almond in color.

To make the lemon curd mousse, in a bowl with an electric mixer, on medium speed, beat the egg yolks and sugar until pale yellow, about 2 minutes. Add the juice, zest, and butter. Transfer to a saucepan. The mixture may appear curdy. Cook over low heat, stirring with a wooden spoon until the mixture becomes smooth and thickens, about 10 minutes. Do not overcook or it will separate. Remove from heat. Pour into a bowl and allow to cool. Cover and refrigerate until you are ready to assemble. (Makes about 1½ cups.)

When you are ready to assemble the cake, whisk the cream in a bowl with an electric mixer until stiff peaks form. Fold in the lemon curd.

To assemble, place a dollop of the mousse on the cake platter. (This will help keep the meringue stable.) Place one of the meringues on the platter, pressing lightly. Spread half the mousse on top of the bottom layer. Add the second meringue and top it with the remaining mousse. Garnish the cake and platter with raspberries and blossoms.

doggy-bones and bathtub bribes

2 cups all-purpose flour

¾ cup whole-wheat flour (see note)

¼ cup cornmeal

1 teaspoon baking soda

2 tablespoons ground ginger

½ teaspoon ground cloves

½ cup molasses

2 tablespoons honey

½ cup water

¼ cup vegetable oil

1 bone-shaped cookie cutter, 5 by 2 inches

1-inch heart-shaped cookie cutter

Everyone needs to be remembered on Valentine's Day, especially your best friend. Three barks for Mo Plummer, who inspired this recipe and owns Portland's Three Dog Bakery. You guessed it: this bakery is devoted to canine confections.

Makes about 4 dozen bones and 8 dozen bribes

Preheat an oven to 375°F. Set aside two greased baking sheets.

In a bowl, whisk together the flours, cornmeal, baking soda, ginger, and cloves. In another bowl, use an electric mixer on low speed to blend the molasses, honey, water, and oil. Add the flour mixture, ½ cup at a time, until blended and no flour shows. With lightly floured hands, gather the dough into a ball. Divide into quarters and flatten each into a disk. Leave one disk out and refrigerate the others, separated with waxed paper or plastic wrap.

On a lightly floured surface, pat and roll out the first disk ⅛ inch thick. Use the bone-shaped cookie cutter to cut the dough into shapes. Use a spatula to transfer the bones onto a baking sheet, leaving ½ inch between them. Bake until set, or until the edges are beginning to color, 8 to 10 minutes. Immediately, take one bone at a time, place it on a work surface, and use the heart-shaped cookie cutter to cut and remove one heart from each end of the bone. The heart cookie will come up with the cutter; pop it out with your fingertip and cool on a wire rack. For crisp biscuits, return the bones to the baking sheet, and bake for 5 more minutes. Repeat rolling, baking, and cutting with the remaining dough. Store in an airtight container for up to 2 weeks, or freeze for up to 2 months.

Note: You can substitute all-purpose flour for the whole-wheat flour and cornmeal.

love potions

Celebrate the day; toast the one you love with these simple and festive Valentine's Day drinks for adults and children. Each of the below recipes makes one serving.

kir royale: adult's version

Pour 1 to 2 tablespoons cassis liqueur in a champagne flute. Fill with champagne and gently stir.

princess royale: kid's version

Pour 1 to 2 tablespoons cassis or raspberry syrup in a champagne flute. Fill with ginger ale and gently stir.

sugar cupid: adult's version

Place one large sugar cube in a glass. Drizzle 1/4 teaspoon grenadine over it. Fill glass 1/2 full with ginger ale or other clear soda pop. Stir in a splash of orange juice and a jigger of bourbon or brandy, and top with ice cubes. Garnish with a spiral twist of orange zest, and serve.

sugar-cube-kid: kid's version

Place one large sugar cube in a glass. Drizzle 1/4 teaspoon grenadine over it. Fill glass 3/4 full with ginger beer or ale. Stir in a splash of orange juice, and top with ice cubes. Garnish with a spiral twist of orange zest, and serve.

Valentine's Day happens only one day a year, but it's fun to celebrate romance and love anytime. One of the nicest ways to show you care is by preparing and sharing a special meal. In this chapter you'll find easy-to-prepare recipes and menus that you and your kids can make together.

valentine menus and recipes

The Sweetheart Breakfast starts the day with warm currant-studded scones, heart-shaped pancakes, and soft-cooked eggs with butter-toasted hearts. A delicious, homemade dinner for two—don't worry, we've got a menu for the cherubs, too—goes together in a heartbeat. You'll discover easy tips for grilling prawns flavored with lemon zest and fennel, the best filet mignon you've ever tasted, and savory potatoes wrapped in parchment with a tiny surprise. And your angels will love a dinner menu designed just for them. There's a spaghetti sauce no kid can resist, a salad dressing they'll all want to make in a jar, and a pink whipped-cream cake that's destined to become a family tradition.

citrus sunrise

For each drink:

1 lime wedge

granulated sugar on a small
plate

1 tablespoon grenadine

6 ounces freshly squeezed
orange juice or combination
of orange, tangerine, and
grapefruit juice

*sweetheart
breakfast menu*

citrus sunrise or
tequila sunrise

sweetheart scones or
chocolate-filled scones

soft-cooked eggs with
butter-toasted hearts or
pitter-patter pancakes

skillet bacon with
brown sugar

french press coffee or
earl grey tea

*For a special wake-up call on a lazy weekend morning, treat your tribe
to this sunny citrus breakfast drink. It's always a hit with the kids: the
sugar-rimmed glass is just-for-fun; the two liquid layers look neat; and
the kids like figuring out how you got the red grenadine syrup to stay
at the bottom. (Grenadine is a heavier liquid.)*

Run the lime wedge around the rim of a stemmed glass. Dip the moist-
ened rim in the sugar. Carefully pour the grenadine into the bottom
of the glass. Along the inside edge of the glass, pour the juice, letting
it rest on top of the grenadine. Serve immediately.

adult version: tequila sunrise

In the sugar-rimmed glass, substitute Chambord, a black raspberry
liqueur, for the grenadine. In a shaker half-filled with ice cubes, combine 1 jigger (1½ ounces or 3 tablespoons) tequila, 1 to 2 tablespoons
triple sec, and the orange juice. Shake well and strain into the glass.

sweetheart scones

A basket of warm and fragrant heart-shaped scones will make sleepy heads rise and shine on February 14. These buttery biscuits, studded with currants and scented with orange zest, are delicious on their own or served with marmalade or jam. If you're an early bird, you can marinate the currants in orange juice for 30 minutes, then strain before adding to the dry ingredients.

Those who are French at heart love to linger over breakfast, especially one that includes warm breakfast bread or croissants filled with bitter-sweet chocolate. Wherever you wake, pretend you're in Paris with the luscious chocolate-filled variation, following page.

Makes 8 to 10 scones

Preheat an oven to 350°F. Set aside a nonstick or parchment–lined baking sheet.

In a bowl, whisk together the flour, sugar, baking powder, and salt until well blended. Using the large holes of a grater, grate the frozen butter into the flour mixture. With a pastry cutter, two knives, or your fingertips, work the pieces into the flour for 30 seconds to 1 minute, until the mixture resembles coarse crumbs. The bits of butter should still be cool to the touch. Toss in the zest and the currants. Combine the egg and half-and-half, and stir into the flour mixture until the dough holds together. Do not overmix.

continued

2 cups all-purpose flour

$1/4$ cup granulated sugar

1 tablespoon baking powder

pinch of salt

6 tablespoons ($3/4$ stick) unsalted
   butter, frozen

1 teaspoon grated or finely
   minced orange zest

$3/4$ cup currants

1 egg, lightly beaten

$3/4$ cup half-and-half

Dust your hands with flour and loosely gather the dough into a ball. Turn it out onto a lightly floured surface. Knead gently two or three times. Lightly pat or roll the dough ½ to ¾ inch thick. Dip a 2½-inch heart or muffin cutter into flour, and cut out the scones. Place on the baking sheet and bake until golden, 12 to 15 minutes. Serve warm.

chocolate-filled scones

Makes about 6 scones

Follow the Sweetheart Scones recipe (page 75), omitting the currants and zest and continuing as directed, rolling the dough 1 inch thick. Cut out six scones with a 2½-inch round biscuit cutter. Bake until golden, about 20 minutes. Immediately make a horizontal slit into each scone, leaving a hinge of crust to hold the two halves together. Insert a portion of bittersweet chocolate bar (I like Perugina, Scharffen Berger, or Lindt) that is slightly larger than the opening, allowing a slip of chocolate to show. Wait 1 minute for the chocolate to slightly warm before serving with a napkin. (The chocolate will retain its shape, until the first bite.)

morning eggs in heart frames

This is one of those kid-can-do recipes that every child enjoys making for breakfast at one time or another. If it's your child's turn to be the morning sous chef at your house, he or she can choose a heart-shaped or any large cookie or muffin cutter. (PS: If you're concerned about stove-top cooking, it's fine to keep the burner on low. The egg will take a little longer to cook and turn out a little harder, but that's okay.)

1 heart-shaped cookie cutter, 3½ by 3 inches

1 slice bread

2 to 4 teaspoons butter, divided

1 egg

Makes 1 serving

Using the cookie cutter, cut a heart-shaped hole in the center of the bread. In a small frying pan, over medium heat, melt 1 to 2 teaspoons of the butter. Add the bread and break the egg into the hole. (It's okay if the yolk breaks.) Cook until the bread is golden brown on the bottom. You can use a spatula to peek under the bread.

Using the spatula, turn the bread and egg over. Add the remaining butter to the pan. Gently lift the bread to make sure the butter gets under the toast, and fry the toast until the egg is done to your liking.

soft-cooked eggs with butter-toasted hearts

Soft-cooked eggs take on an interesting personality when their shells are covered with tiny red hearts and they're served with butter-toasted hearts. Your children will want to help you make—and eat—this breakfast. They can decorate the eggs and cut the toast. Just remember to tell them not to squeeze the uncooked eggs too tightly or you'll end up making scrambled eggs instead.

You will need:

fresh eggs
red felt-tipped permanent pen
sliced bread
butter, at room temperature

Remove the eggs from the refrigerator 30 minutes before preparing. (The eggs need to be at room temperature before decorating; otherwise, the ink will not adhere to the shells. This also helps to keep the eggs from cracking while cooking.) Use a soft towel to carefully dry each egg. Using the pen, cover each eggshell with tiny hearts. Set the eggs aside to let the ink dry completely while bringing a pot of cold water to a simmer. Be sure the saucepan is large enough so that the eggs aren't crowded. Place the eggs in the water. From the moment the water begins to simmer again, time the cooking. For firm whites, but still liquid yolks, boil for 2 to 3 minutes, depending on egg size. For firmer yolks that will hold their shape, cook for 4 to 6 minutes.

To make the toast, depending on your preference, you can butter the bread slices before or after you toast them. Once a slice is toasted, use the largest heart-shaped cookie cutter you have to stamp out a heart-shaped piece.

pitter-patter pancakes

Little hearts will flip over these fun and easy breakfast cakes, made by pouring pancake batter into heart-shaped cookie cutters. Your babes can help get the cookie cutters ready for the griddle by attaching wooden clothespins to act as handles.

You will need:

5-inch heart-shaped cookie cutter

cooking oil spray

wooden clothespin

your favorite pancake recipe

Spray the inside of the cookie cutter with cooking oil. Clip the clothespin onto the cookie cutter to act as a wooden handle. Make your favorite pancake batter. Place the cookie cutter on a hot griddle or skillet and pour in 3 to 4 tablespoons batter. Cook until the top is bubbly and the cake is dry around the edges. When your heart is ready to flip, use the cool wooden handle to lift and remove the cookie cutter. (It should slip off easily by itself, or with a light touch.) Turn and cook until golden on the second side and serve.

skillet bacon with brown sugar

Everything tastes better with bacon, especially when the bacon is crispy brown and gleaming with caramelized sugar.

$\frac{1}{2}$ pound sliced bacon

1 tablespoon brown sugar

Serves 2

Add the bacon to a cold skillet over medium-low heat. When it begins to soften and sizzle, separate the slices with a fork and regulate the heat to make sure that the slices brown evenly, turning frequently. If too much fat is present, pour off the drippings. When the bacon is almost crisp, sprinkle with the sugar and continue to fry until the sugar has melted, about 1 minute. Drain on paper towels and serve.

hearts-on-fire grilled prawns

8 jumbo prawns or shrimps (total 10 to 16 ounces), shelled and deveined with tails on

3 teaspoons fennel seeds, roasted and ground (see note)

2 teaspoons minced or grated lemon zest

$\frac{1}{2}$ teaspoon lemon pepper

pinch of cayenne pepper

pernod or olive oil for drizzling

3 ounces chevre, cut into four $\frac{1}{4}$-inch slices

$\frac{1}{4}$ cup red pepper sauce or puree

herb sprigs for garnishing, such as feathery anise or flat-leaf parsley

dinner-for-two menu

kir royale (page 71)

hearts-on-fire grilled prawns

filet mignon with four butters

savory-scented potatoes in parchment

spinach salad with pear, gorgonzola, and toasted pecans

bergamot panna cotta

With this elegant and easy first course, grilled prawns take on the lovely taste of lemon zest and fennel.

Serves 4

Place each prawn flat on a cutting board. Butterfly by holding a knife parallel to the surface and slicing the prawn almost through, starting at the head and stopping at the tail. Don't cut through the tail. Open the prawn so that it lies flat. Repeat with remaining prawns.

In a small bowl, combine the fennel, lemon zest, lemon pepper, and cayenne. Drizzle the prawns with Pernod. Shake off excess liquid, and coat each prawn with the spice mixture. Place the prawns in a shallow dish and marinate at room temperature for 1 hour.

Preheat the broiler on medium, or use an outdoor grill with very hot coals. Set the rack about 4 inches from the element or coals. To keep the prawns from curling, run two 10-inch wooden skewers through each prawn in an X, starting at the tail and emerging at the head at the opposite side. Broil or grill for 2 to 2½ minutes per side, depending on size. The interior meat will be opaque when done.

To serve, remove the skewers from the prawns. Arrange a slice of chevre in the center of four plates. Drizzle the red pepper sauce around it. Encircle two prawns around the cheese or rest them together at the side. If desired, sprinkle a few drops of Pernod on each prawn. Garnish with an herb sprig.

Note: Roast fennel seeds in a small dry saucepan, over medium heat, stirring occasionally until brown, about 3 minutes. Remove from heat, and cool for 5 minutes. To grind, use a mortar and pestle, or a clean electric coffee grinder.

filet mignon with four butters

One way to enhance the great flavor of filet mignon is to rub the meat with salt and pepper and olive oil. I learned this tip from meat guru Bruce Aidells. For special occasions, I like to treat myself and Pete to a choice of flavored butters to go along with the filet. A dollop on top of a steak melts into a rich and delicious sauce. I've included four of our favorites.

Serves 2

5 tablespoons extra-virgin olive oil

2 teaspoons kosher salt

1 tablespoon freshly ground black pepper

2 filet mignon steaks, each 1½ inches thick

4 to 6 teaspoons flavored butters (recipes follow)

In a small bowl, stir together 3 tablespoons of the olive oil, and the salt and pepper. Rub the mixture over the steaks. Place the steaks in a shallow bowl and cover with plastic wrap. Marinate in the refrigerator for 2 hours or overnight.

Remove the steaks from the refrigerator 1 hour before cooking so they can reach room temperature. Preheat an oven to 350°F.

In a heavy cast-iron skillet, over medium-high heat, heat the remaining 2 tablespoons olive oil for 1 minute. Fry the steaks for 4 minutes on each side. To sear the edges, use tongs to hold the steaks' edges against the hot skillet for the first minute.

Place the skillet and steaks in the oven. For medium rare, bake for 15 minutes, or until an instant-read thermometer reads 125°F to 130°F. Use an oven mitt to remove the skillet. Remove the steaks to a platter and let them rest for 5 to 7 minutes so that the meat juices can redistribute and the residual heat can finish cooking the steaks.

To serve, top each steak with 2 to 3 teaspoons of the lemon-parsley butter, caper butter, garlic butter, or horseradish butter (page 85), or pass the butters separately on the side.

lemon-parsley butter

In a bowl, mix together ¼ cup room-temperature unsalted butter,
1 tablespoon finely chopped parsley, 1 to 2 teaspoons lemon juice,
and ¼ teaspoon salt. Keep at room temperature if you are going to use
within 2 hours. Otherwise, use plastic wrap to shape it into a roll and
refrigerate for up to 1 week. To use, slice off 2 to 3 teaspoons per steak.

caper butter

In a processor or a bowl, use a hand blender to process ¼ cup unsalted
butter, 1½ teaspoons capers, 1 to 2 anchovy fillets, 1 tablespoon lemon
juice, and leaves from 3 sprigs of flat-leaf parsley until smooth. Season
with salt and pepper. Keep at room temperature if you are going to use
within 2 hours. Otherwise, store as directed above.

garlic butter

In a bowl, mix together ¼ cup room-temperature unsalted butter, 1 tablespoon finely chopped garlic, ½ teaspoon dried and crushed rosemary,
and ¼ teaspoon salt. Keep at room temperature if you are going to use
within 2 hours. Otherwise, store as directed above.

horseradish butter

In a bowl, mix together ¼ cup room-temperature unsalted butter, 1 tablespoon drained, prepared horseradish, 2 teaspoons chopped fresh parsley,
and ¼ teaspoon salt. Keep at room temperature if you are going to
use within 2 hours. Otherwise, store as directed above.

excellent

spinach salad with pear, gorgonzola, and toasted pecans

½ cup vegetable oil

⅓ cup seasoned rice vinegar

2 tablespoons fresh lime juice

4 cups (about 6 ounces) baby spinach, stems removed

1 ripe pear, peeled, cored, and cubed

½ cup (about 2 ounces) crumbled Gorgonzola cheese

⅓ cup chopped toasted pecans (see note)

In this salad, the sum is even greater than the parts. Three simple ingredients—vegetable oil, rice vinegar, and fresh lime juice—are all you need to create the fresh-tasting dressing for this irresistibly delicious spinach salad.

Serves 4

In a bowl, whisk together the oil, vinegar, and lime juice until combined.

In a salad bowl, place the spinach and pear. Toss with enough dressing to coat. Sprinkle the cheese and pecans over the salad, and serve immediately. Pass any remaining dressing.

Note: You can purchase pecans bits or chop your own. To toast, preheat an oven to 350°F and spread the nuts on a rimmed baking sheet. Bake until golden, 5 to 7 minutes, watching carefully.

savory-scented potatoes
in parchment

Good things often come in small packages, and it's certainly true when baby new potatoes are combined with olive oil, garlic, and rosemary, and wrapped in parchment paper hearts. Cooking in parchment seals in all those wonderful flavors. You'll enjoy these potatoes from the moment you open your fragrant and savory package.

If valentines are on your mind, tuck some tiny heart-shaped carrot slices inside the packets before baking. They're always a delight to discover.

Serves 4

Preheat an oven to 350°F. Fold each sheet of parchment in half by bringing the short ends together. With scissors, trim the unfolded edges of each sheet to form a half-heart shape. Unfold the papers and set aside.

In a bowl, stir together the olive oil, new potatoes, garlic, salt, and pepper.

Divide the potato mixture among the parchment papers, placing the mixture to one side of the fold line. Make sure each portion has 1 or 2 cloves of garlic. Add a sprig of rosemary to each packet, and heart-shaped carrots, if desired. Fold the empty halves of the parchment over the potatoes. Beginning with a folded corner, twist and fold the edges of each paper together and seal the ends by twisting them. You will have four half-heart-shaped packets. Place the packets on a baking sheet and bake for 20 minutes.

To serve, place each packet on a plate and slit the packets open at the table.

4 sheets parchment paper, each 14 by 8 inches

2 tablespoons olive oil

1 pound small, firm new potatoes, whole or cut into 1½-inch cubes

4 to 8 small cloves garlic, peeled

kosher salt and pepper to taste

4 sprigs fresh rosemary

16 heart-shaped carrot slices (optional, page 61)

bergamot panna cotta

Smooth and creamy custard-like panna cotta *is the quintessential Italian dessert. It's also very easy to make. The classic flavor is almond or vanilla. In our recipe, we use bergamot, a provocative citrus essence found in Earl Grey tea. Steeping the tea bags with the heavy cream releases the flavors and gives this dessert its creamy almond color.*

Serves 4

Set aside four stemmed glasses, lightly buttered heart-shaped molds, or ramekins. In a small bowl or glass measuring cup, sprinkle the gelatin over the milk. Let it stand until the gelatin softens and absorbs the milk, 2 to 3 minutes. Lightly stir to break up the gelatin.

In a medium saucepan, over medium-low heat, combine the cream, sugar, and tea bags, stirring occasionally, until the mixture just reaches a boil. (Be sure to stir gently to avoid ripping the tea bags.) Remove from heat. You may notice some tiny black flecks resembling vanilla beans. This is tea dust, and it's just fine. Lightly squeeze the tea bags into the cream to release more of the tea color and flavor; discard bags. (A light squeezing will not release any bitter tannins.) Whisk in the milk mixture until the gelatin is completely dissolved. Briefly reheat the mixture over low heat, if necessary. Stir in the vanilla. Pour the mixture into a pitcher. Fill the glasses or molds. Refrigerate until set, 3 to 4 hours or overnight.

To serve, present the dessert in a stemmed glass by itself or topped with fruit. To serve unmolded, run a sharp knife along the inside of each mold and dip the bottom of the mold into a bowl of hot water. Place a plate over the mold and invert, tapping the bottom if necessary. Top with the berries, raspberry sauce, or dried cherries, and sift powdered sugar over the top, if desired.

1 package (2 teaspoons) unflavored gelatin

1 cup whole milk or half-and-half

1 cup heavy (whipping) cream

$\frac{1}{2}$ cup powdered sugar

3 earl grey tea bags

$\frac{1}{2}$ teaspoon vanilla extract

assortment of fresh berries, raspberry sauce, or dried cherries marinated in brandy, as a topping, powdered sugar (optional)

kids' favorite spaghetti sauce

Back in the days when Frankie Avalon and Annette Funicello were an item, this was my favorite spaghetti sauce. I loved it chunky. Whenever Brad Pitt met his newest flame, my daughter Julie consoled herself with the same sauce, but smooth. (She didn't think *she liked onions and carrots. Hooray for the hand blender.) These days, her three-year-old son Dylan Paul doesn't care who Tarzan likes, but he sure does love this spaghetti sauce, chunky or smooth. Your kids will too.*

Makes about 8 cups

In a skillet, over medium heat, brown the ground beef and sausage. (You won't need any additional fat; the sausage will provide enough.) Use a wooden spoon to crumble and mix the meats.

Meanwhile, in a Dutch oven over medium heat, add the oil and onion and sauté until onion is limp, about 5 minutes. Add the garlic, celery, and carrots and continue to sauté for 3 minutes. Stir in the oregano, basil, celery salt, red pepper flakes, and paprika and continue to sauté for 2 minutes.

Using a slotted spoon, transfer the browned meat into the Dutch oven. Stir in the tomato sauce, juice, and paste; wine; and water. Bring the mixture to a boil. Turn the heat to low and continue to simmer, uncovered, for 30 minutes. Turn off the heat, cover, and let the sauce cool to room temperature. If desired, use a hand blender to pulse the sauce several times for a smoother consistency. Reheat and serve over your favorite pasta. Refrigerate for up to 3 days, or freeze for up to 4 months.

1 pound lean ground beef

1 pound Italian chicken sausage

2 tablespoons olive oil

1 to 1½ cups chopped onion

3 cloves minced garlic

2 medium celery ribs, diced

2 carrots, peeled and shredded

1 tablespoon dried oregano leaves

1 tablespoon dried basil leaves

1 teaspoon celery salt

½ teaspoon dried red pepper flakes

1 teaspoon paprika

1 can (14 ounces) tomato sauce

1 can (11½ ounces) tomato juice

1 can (6 ounces) tomato paste

¼ cup red table wine (optional)

½ cup water

little cherubs' menu

kids' favorite spaghetti sauce with pasta

tossed green salad with shake-it-baby dressing

oh-ma's pink whipped-cream cake

shake-it-baby salad dressing

excellent

3½ T.

H.

½ lemon

1 t

½ t.

½ T.

¼ cup plus 2 tablespoons vegetable oil or extra-virgin olive oil

2 tablespoons white wine vinegar, plain or herb-flavored

juice from 1 large lemon

2 teaspoons Dijon-style mustard or 1 teaspoon dry mustard

1 teaspoon garlic-and-parsley salt

1 tablespoon granulated sugar

optional additions and combinations:

1 large clove garlic, pressed or finely minced, and/or

½ cup grated Parmesan cheese, and/or

¼ cup finely minced fresh herb leaves, and/or

1 tablespoon heavy (whipping) cream

This is the first salad dressing I remember making. I was about six years old and it always seemed a bit like magic, pouring all those different ingredients together. With an "Abracadabra" and a few hefty shakes, they were ready to dress a bowl of fresh salad greens.

In those days, flavorful olive oils and Dijon mustards were few and far between. Instead, clear, flavorless vegetable oil, dry mustards, and garlic salt ruled the day. I still think they make a terrific salad dressing, although, over the years, I've added the Dijon.

Let your kids shake it up and create their own special dressing by adding one or more of the optional ingredients.

Makes about ¾ cup

In a jar, combine the oil, vinegar, lemon juice, mustard, salt, sugar, and any additional options you choose. Screw on the lid and shake, rattle, and roll really well. Or, simply shake the jar until the mixture is well blended.

To serve, drizzle over salad greens and toss, or serve separately, and let everyone use as much as he or she wants.

oh-ma's pink whipped-cream cake

Many grown-ups shy away at the sight of a pink cake, especially one that's flavored with a gelatin dessert. But that's okay. It leaves more for us kids to enjoy. Little do those big guys know, Oh-Ma's pink cake is like a wonderful pound cake that's just right with a simple dusting of powdered sugar.

I confess I'm known as "Oh-Ma" to my three-year-old grandson Dylan, and for a super Valentine's Day celebration, I'll cover the cake with a chilled pink whipped-cream topping garnished with red candy hearts, jelly beans, and pink and white animal crackers. We're hoping all that stuff keeps the grown-ups away, but it doesn't work for long. Once they get a bite, they want their own slice.

Makes one 8-inch cake; serves 4 to 6

Chill a bowl and beaters for 15 to 30 minutes. Preheat an oven to 350°F. Spray an 8-inch springform pan with vegetable cooking spray. Fit a circle of parchment or waxed paper in the bottom, and spray the sheet with oil; set aside.

In a bowl, whisk together the flour, baking powder, and salt.

In the chilled bowl, sprinkle the granulated gelatin over the cream and beat until stiff peaks form. Add the eggs, one at a time, and beat until the mixture is light, about 1 minute. Beat in the sugar, lemon zest, and vanilla. Slowly add the flour mixture to the cream mixture and continue to beat until combined.

Pour the batter into the pan. Bake until the top is golden brown and a toothpick inserted into the middle comes out clean, about 35 minutes. Remove and let cool in the pan, then remove the sides.

continued

For the cake:

1½ cups cake flour

2 teaspoons baking powder

¼ teaspoon salt

2 tablespoons strawberry-banana-flavored powdered gelatin dessert

1 cup chilled heavy (whipping) cream

2 eggs, lightly beaten

1 cup granulated sugar

lemon zest

1 teaspoon vanilla extract

For the topping:

2 tablespoons strawberry-banana-flavored powdered gelatin dessert

¼ cup powdered sugar

¾ cup chilled heavy (whipping) cream

½ teaspoon vanilla extract

red candy hearts, jelly beans, and/or animal crackers for garnishing (optional)

To make the topping, chill a bowl and beaters for 15 to 30 minutes. In the chilled bowl, sprinkle the granulated gelatin and powdered sugar over the cream. Add the vanilla. Beat until stiff peaks form.

To assemble, place a dollop of the topping on a cake platter. (This will help keep the cake in place.) Place the cake on the platter, pressing lightly. Spread the topping on top and on the sides, if desired. Garnish the top with candy hearts, jelly beans, and/or animal crackers, if desired.

pete's favorite almond cake

My husband, Pete, asked me to include this variation. He says, "This is my favorite cake. Period."

Follow Oh-Ma's Pink Whipped-Cream Cake recipe, omitting the powdered gelatin and substituting 1½ teaspoons almond extract for the 1 teaspoon vanilla extract. After removing the cake from the oven, dust only with powdered sugar. Serve plain or with fresh berries and slightly sweetened whipped cream.

index